Mandala Patterns Coloring book
for Kids and Adults

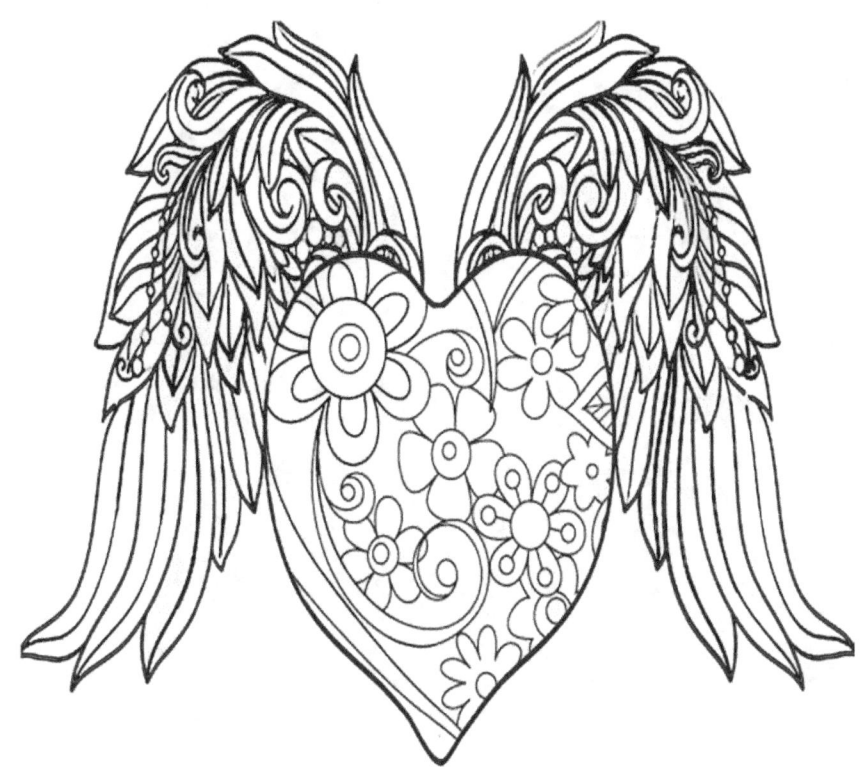

Nina Packer

Mandalas Patterns Coloring book for Kids and Adults

ISBN-13: 978-1983769832

ISBN-10: 1983769835

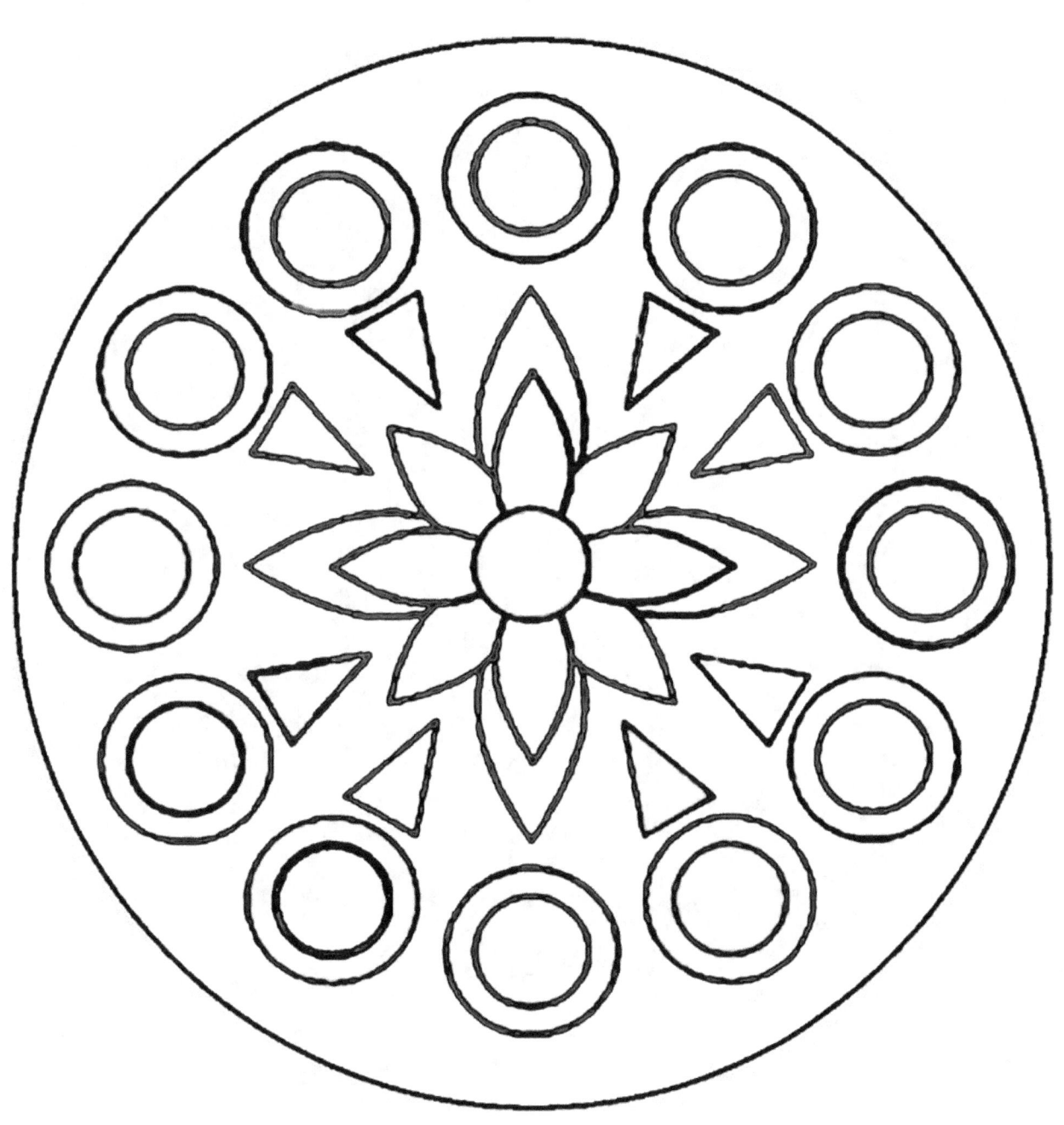

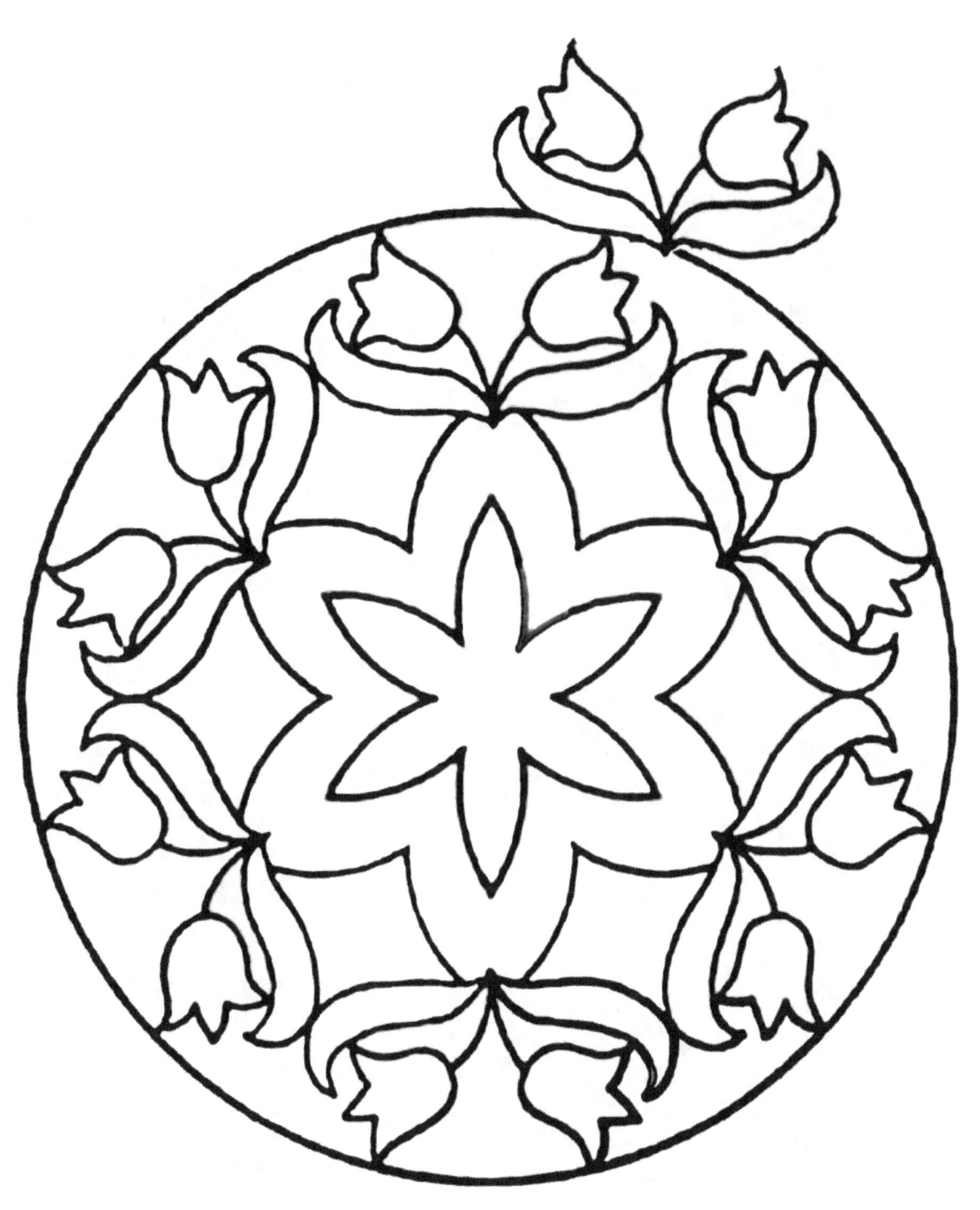

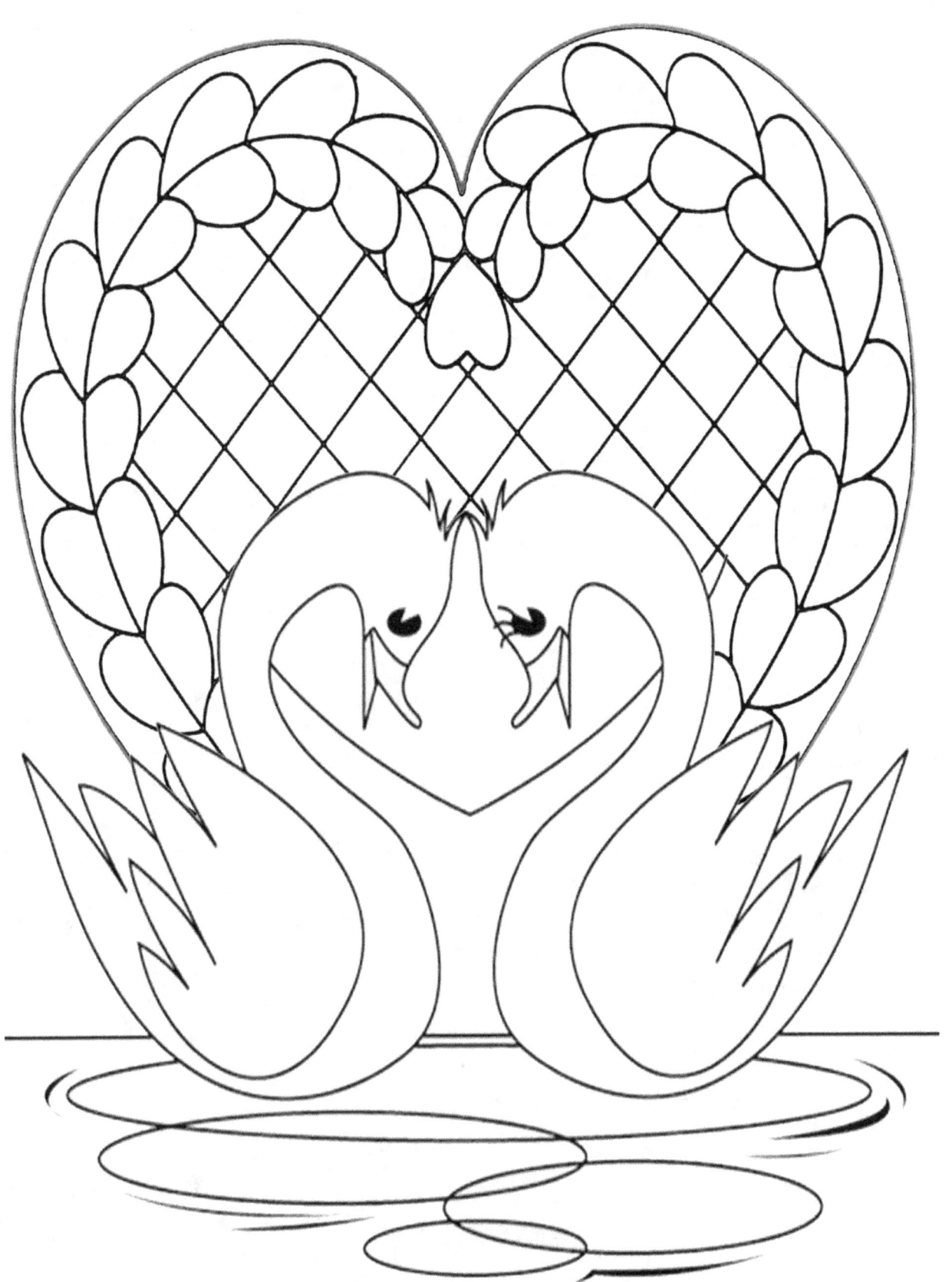

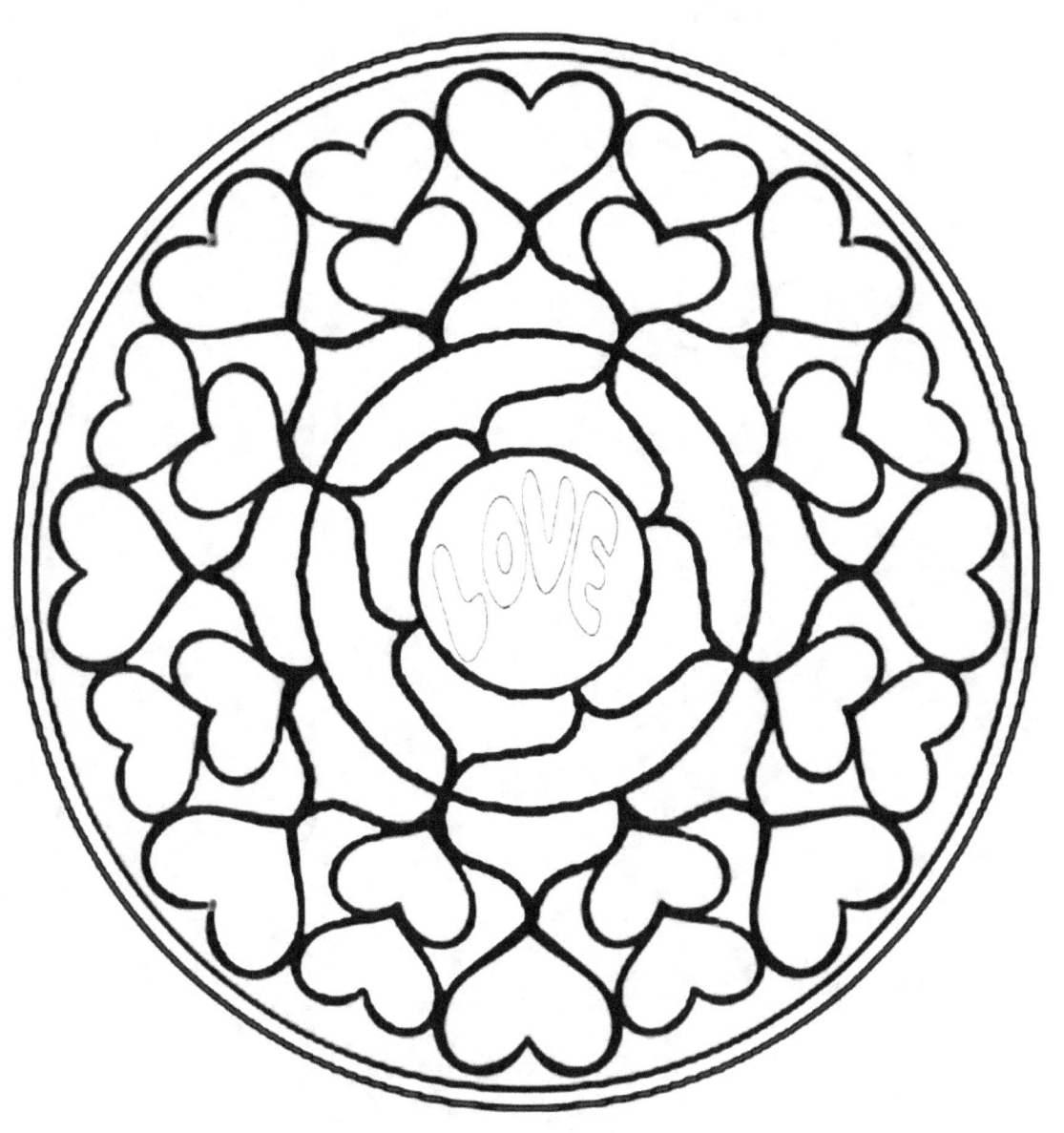

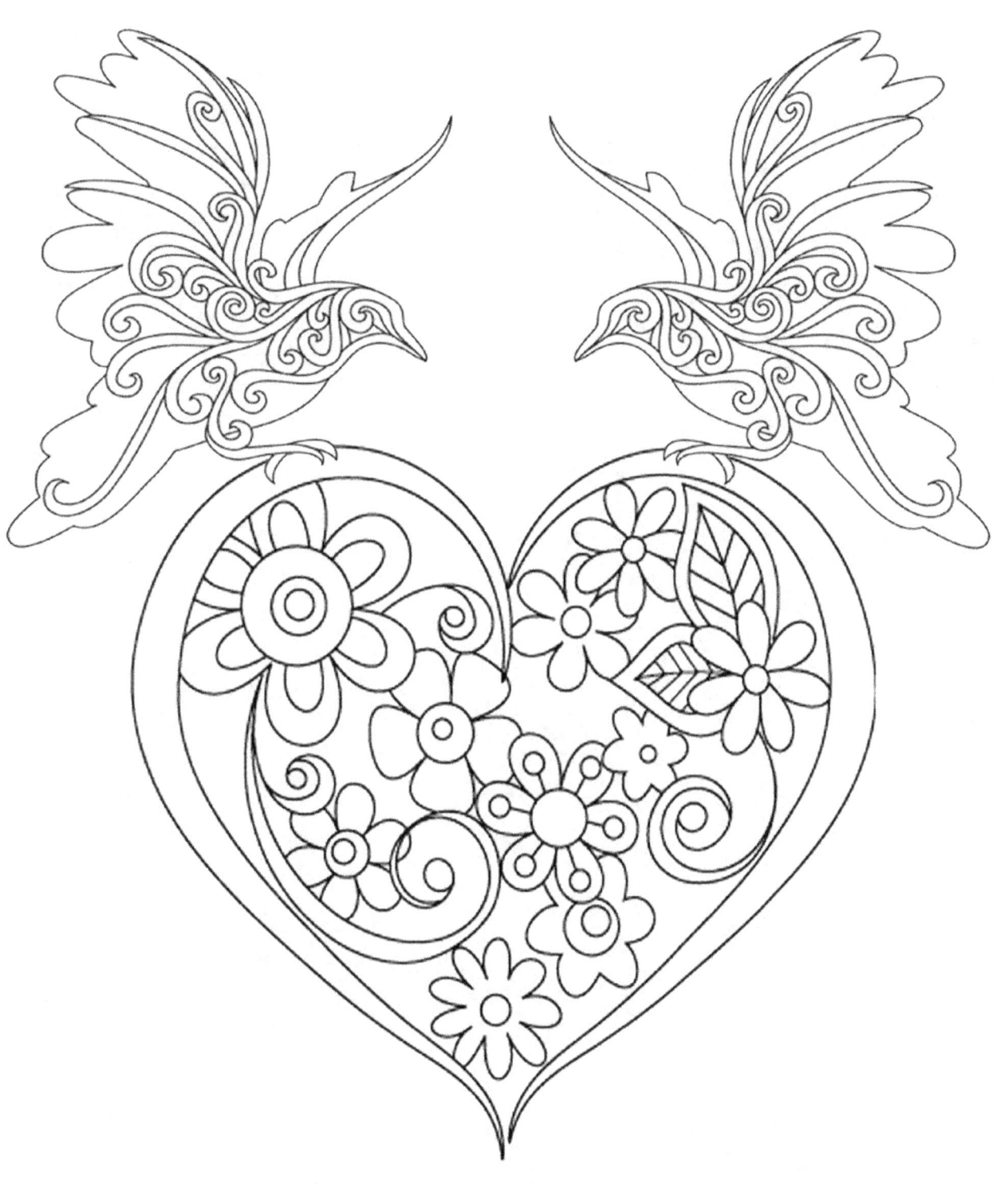

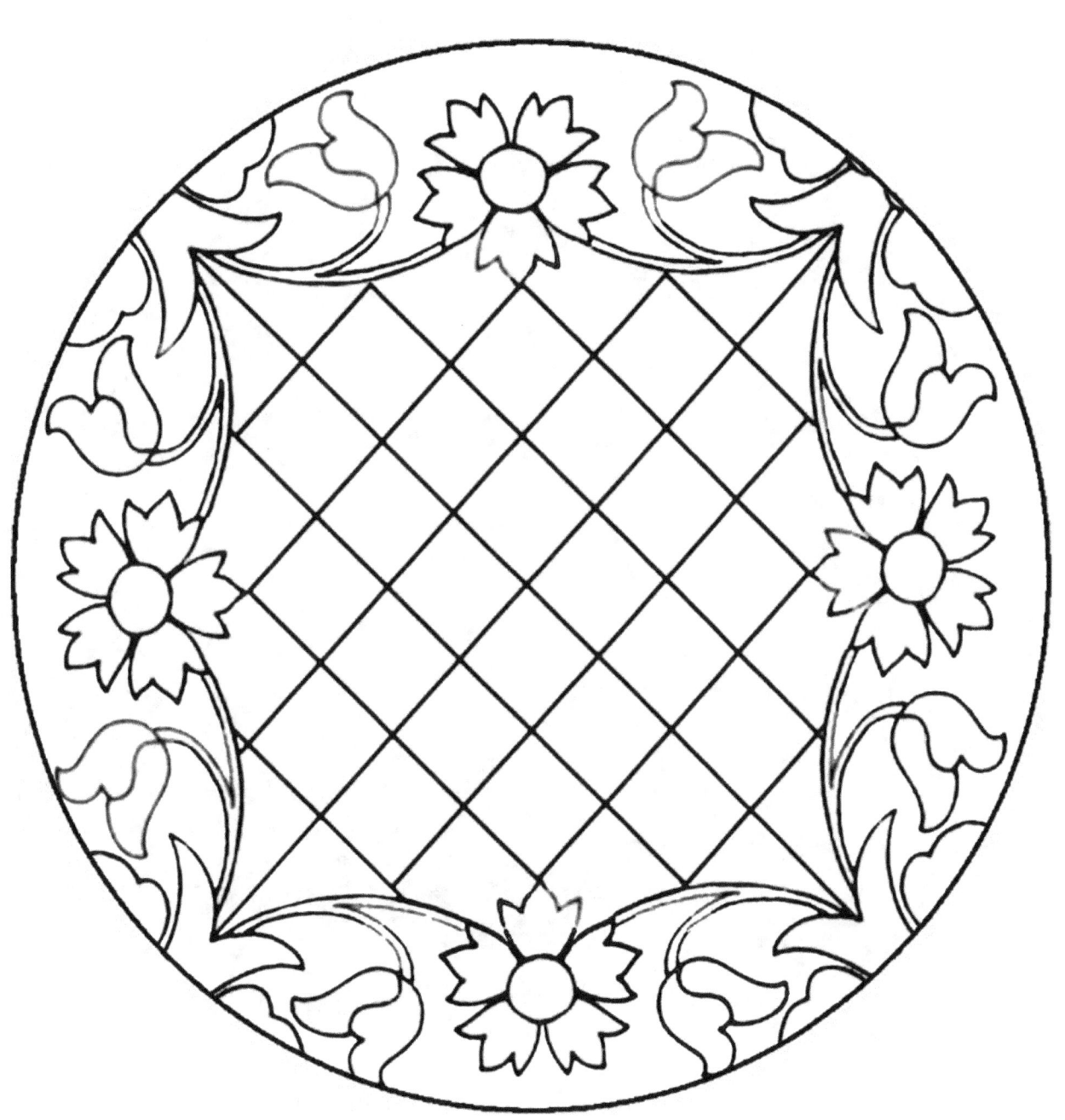

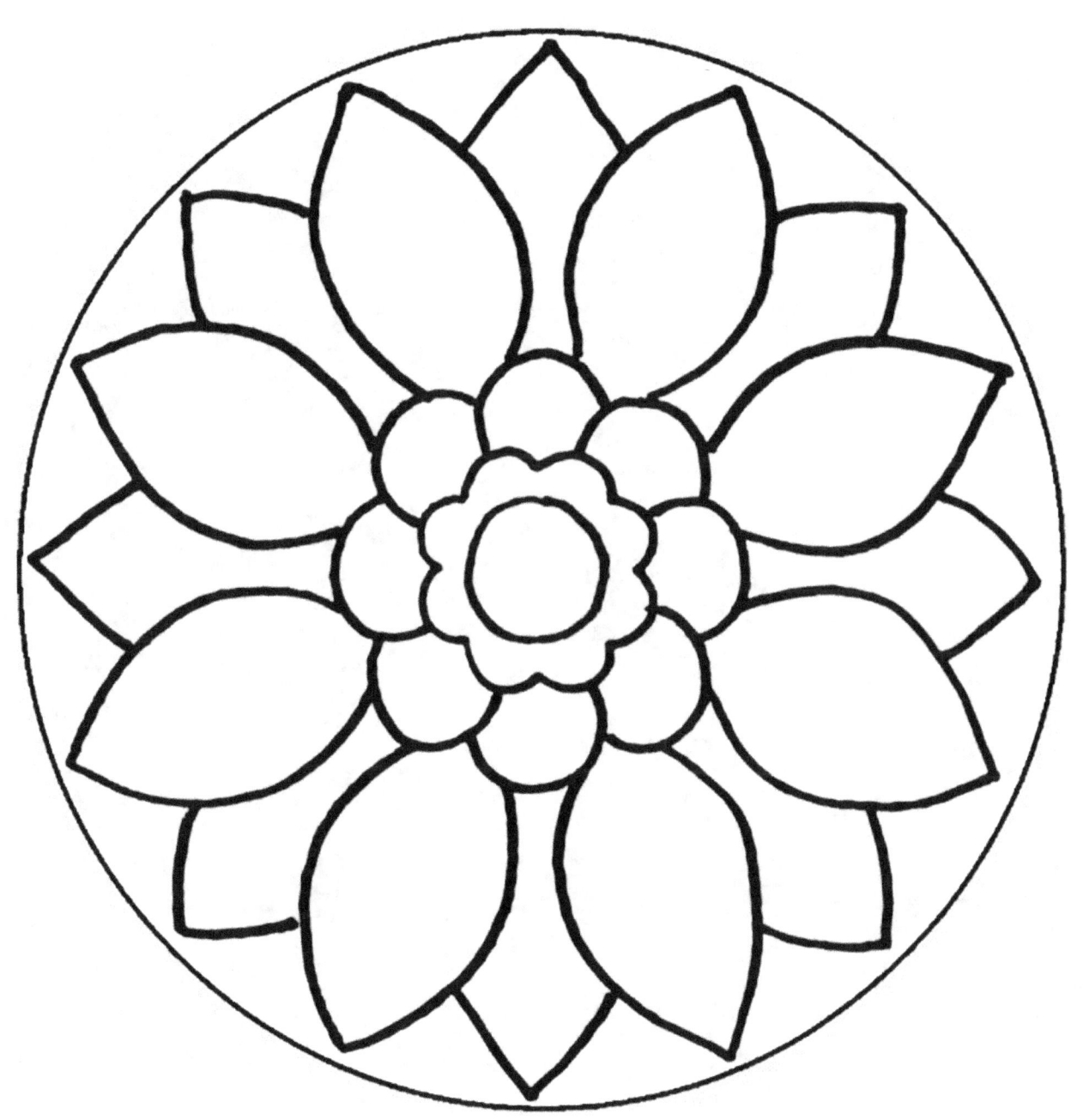

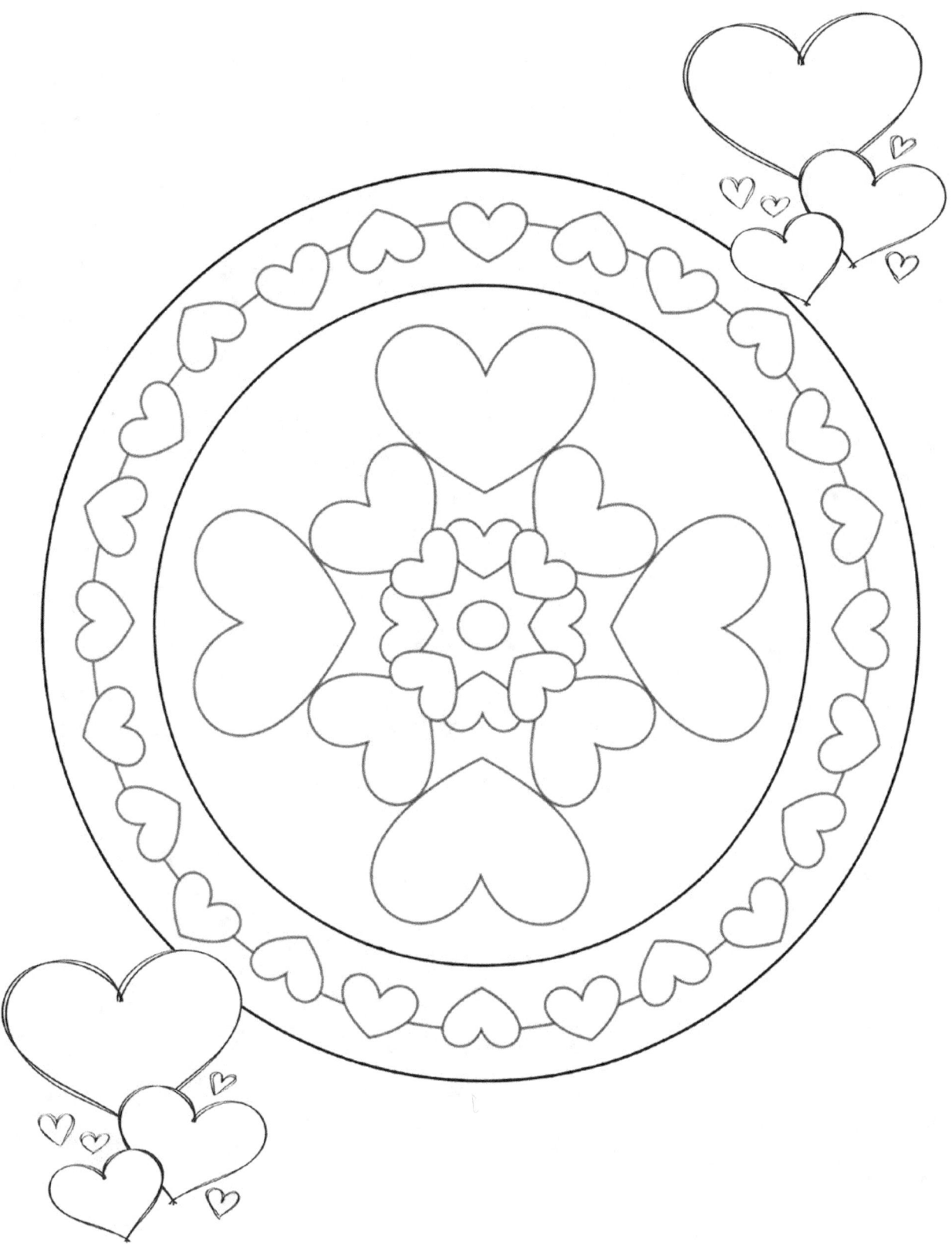

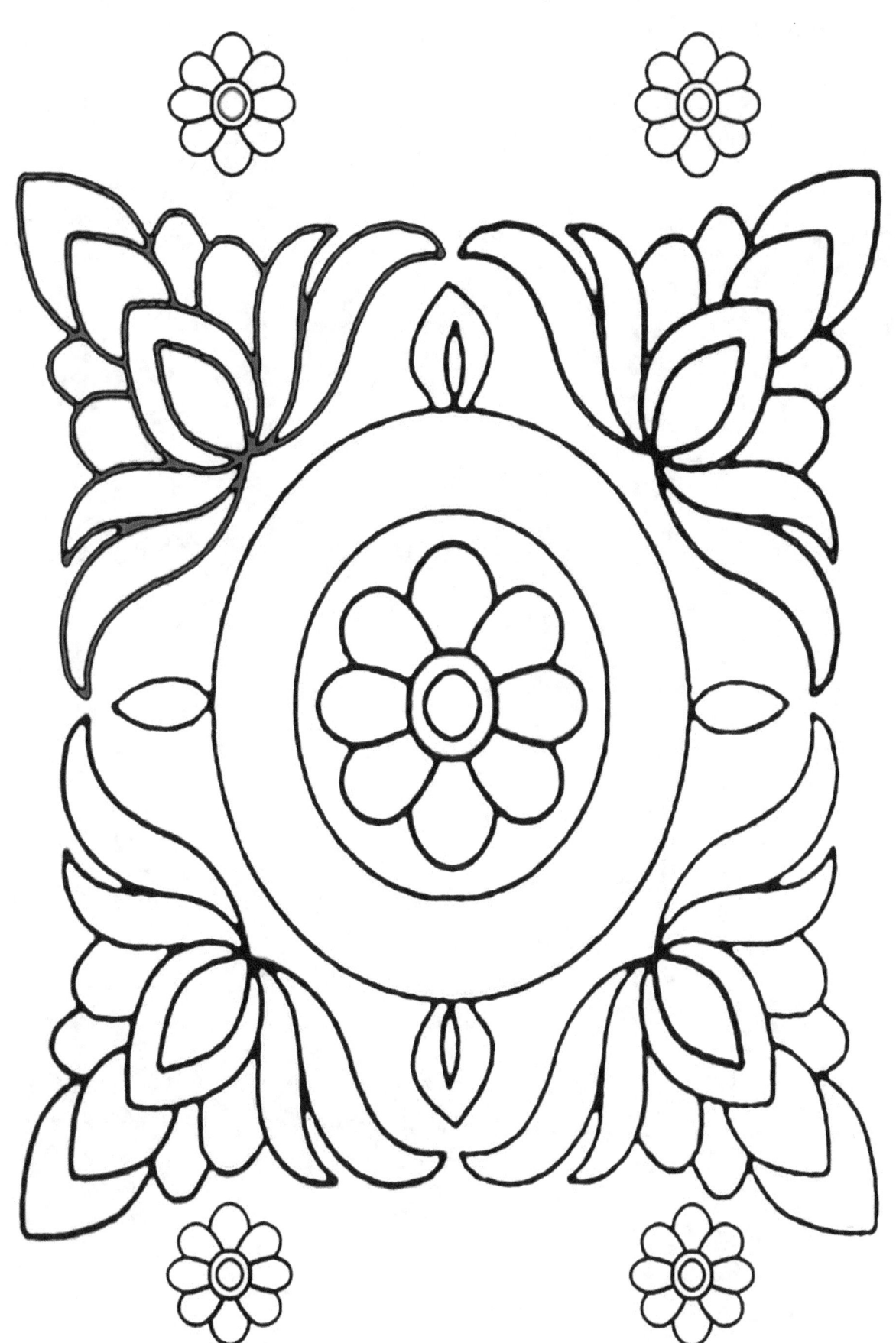

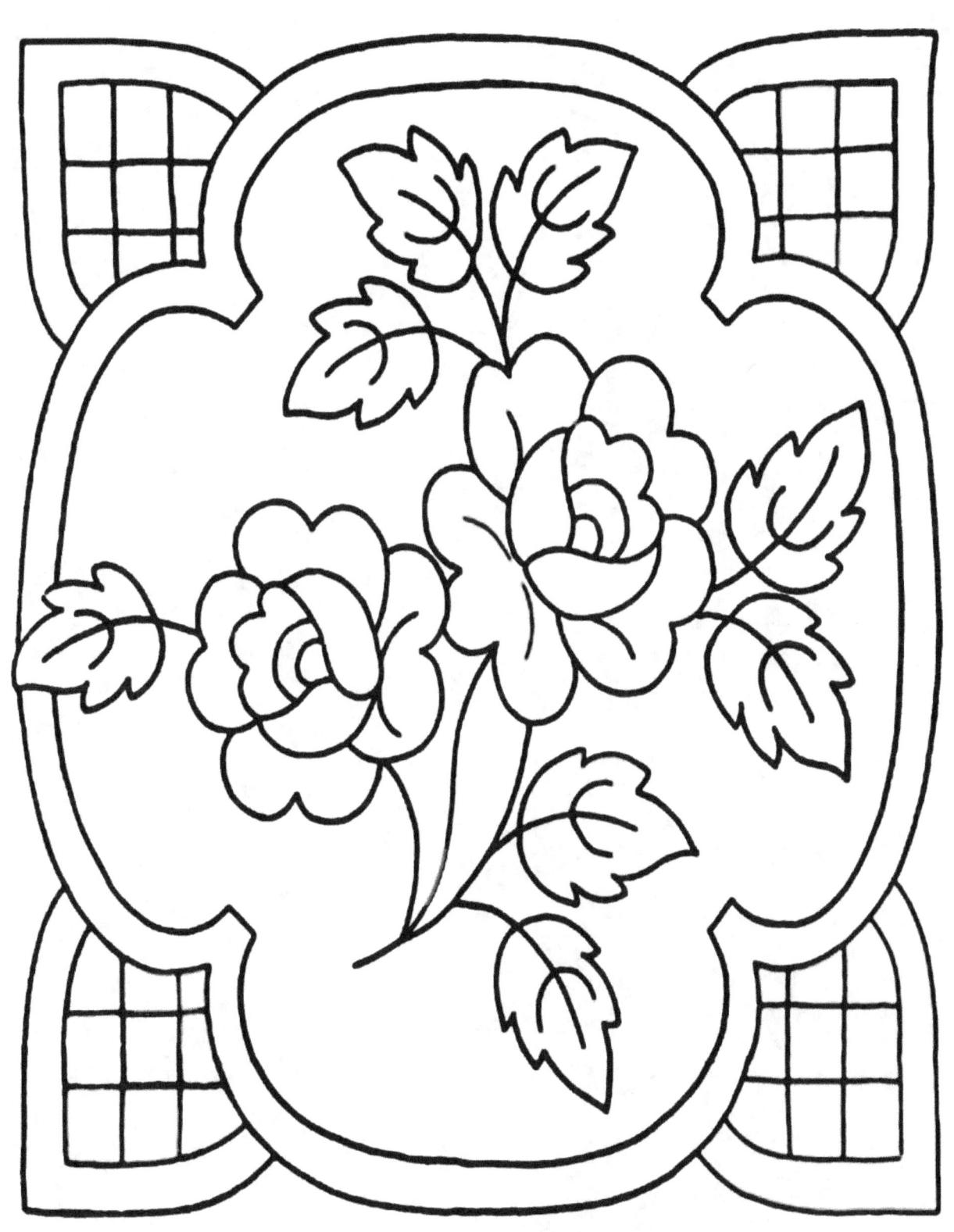

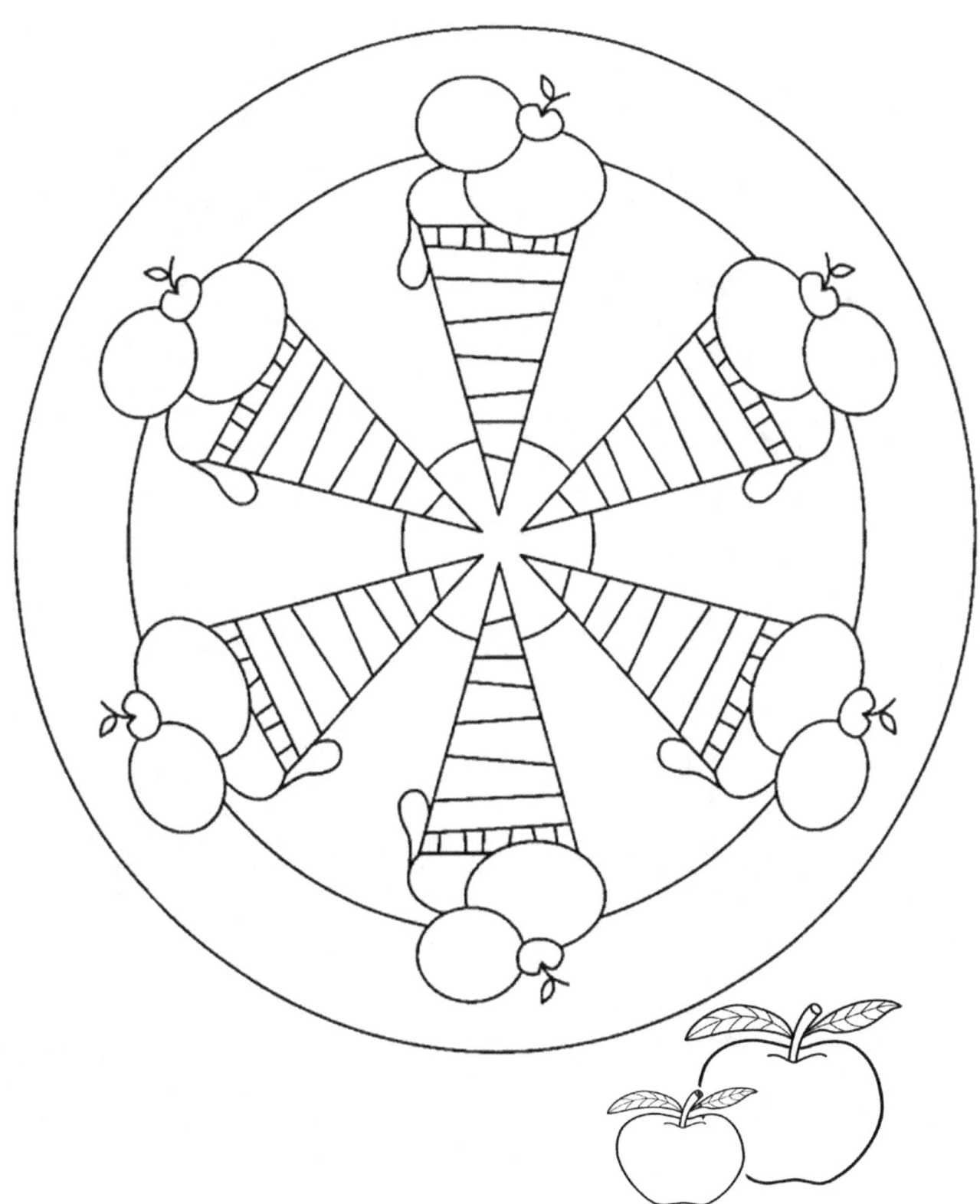

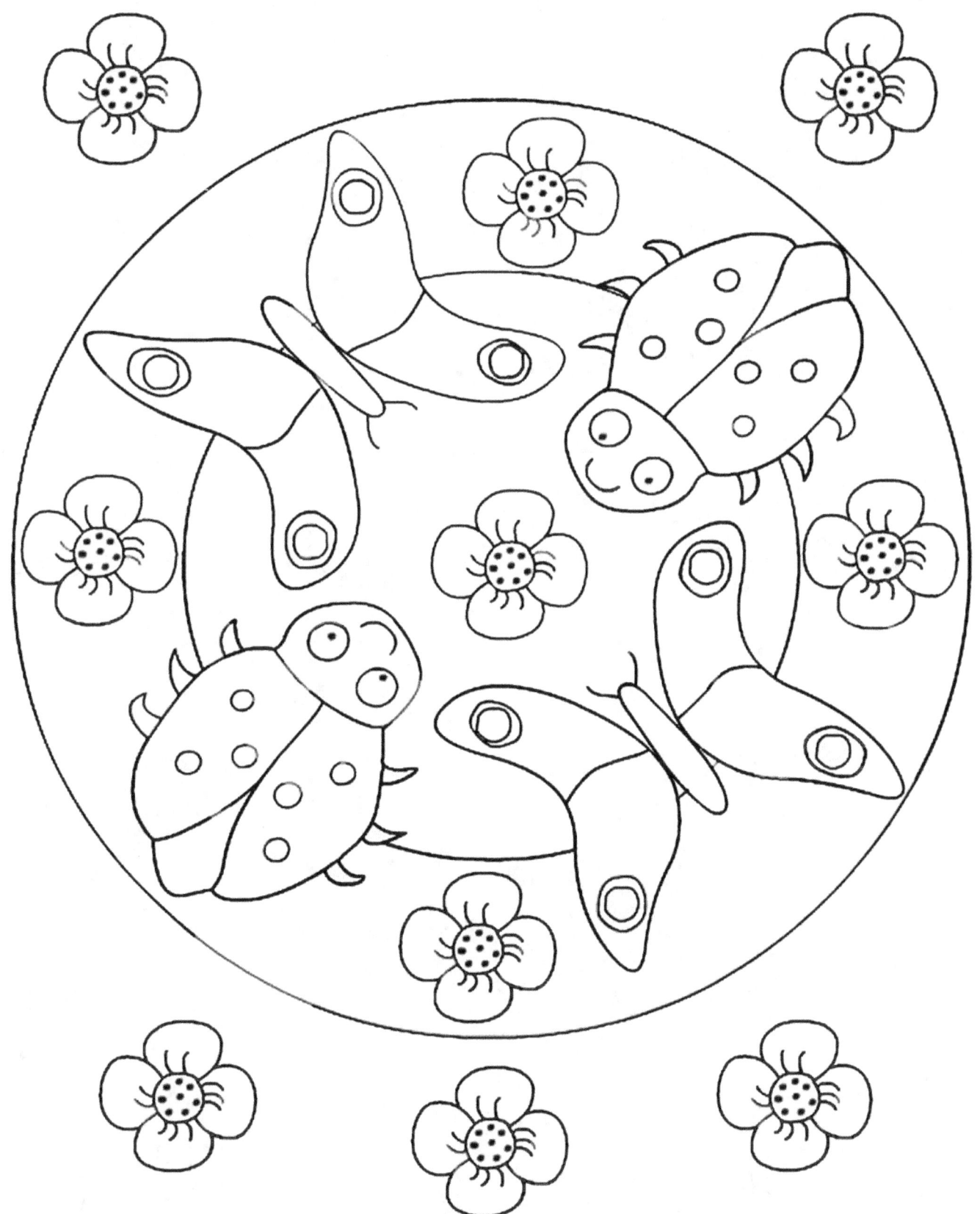

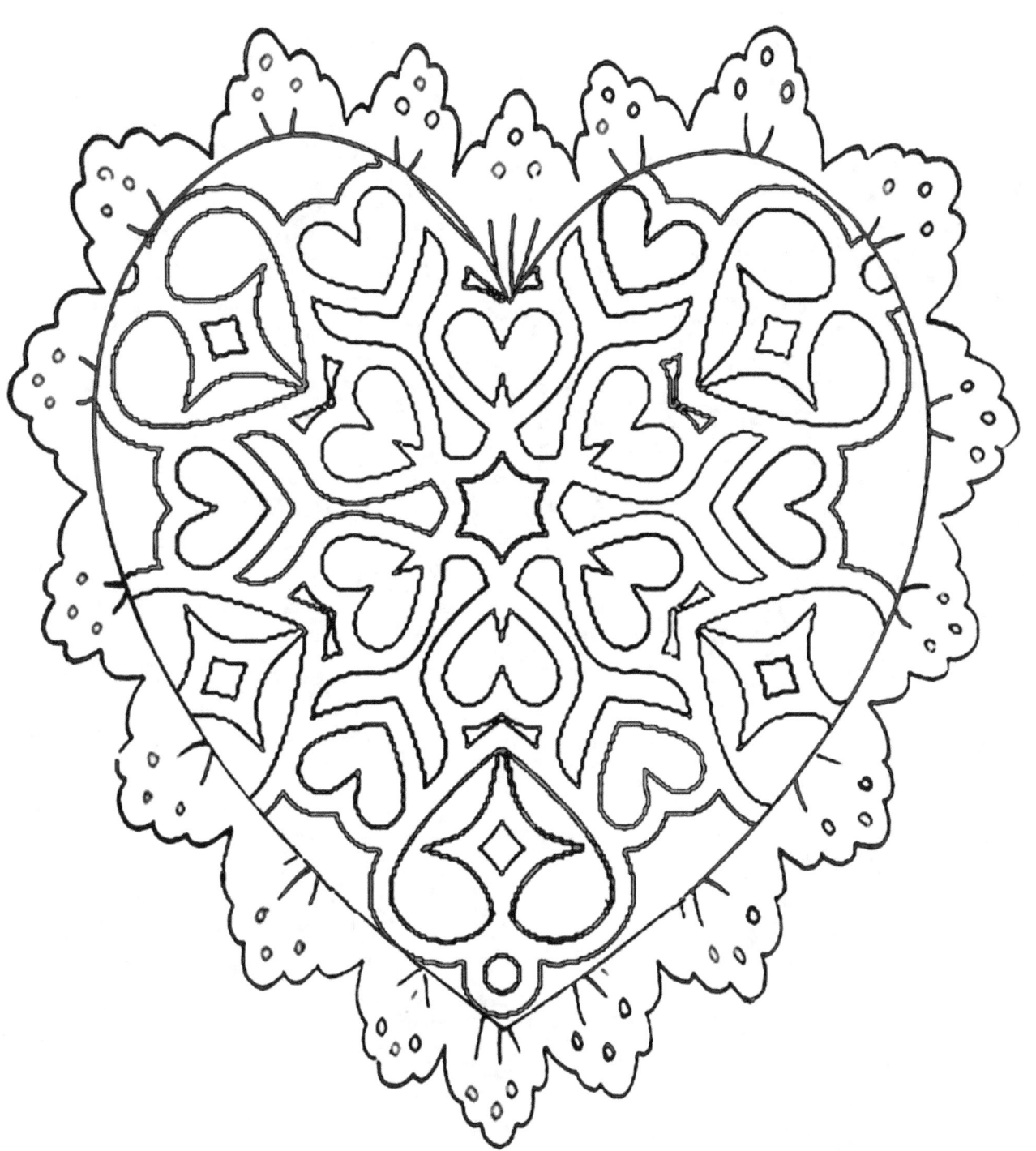

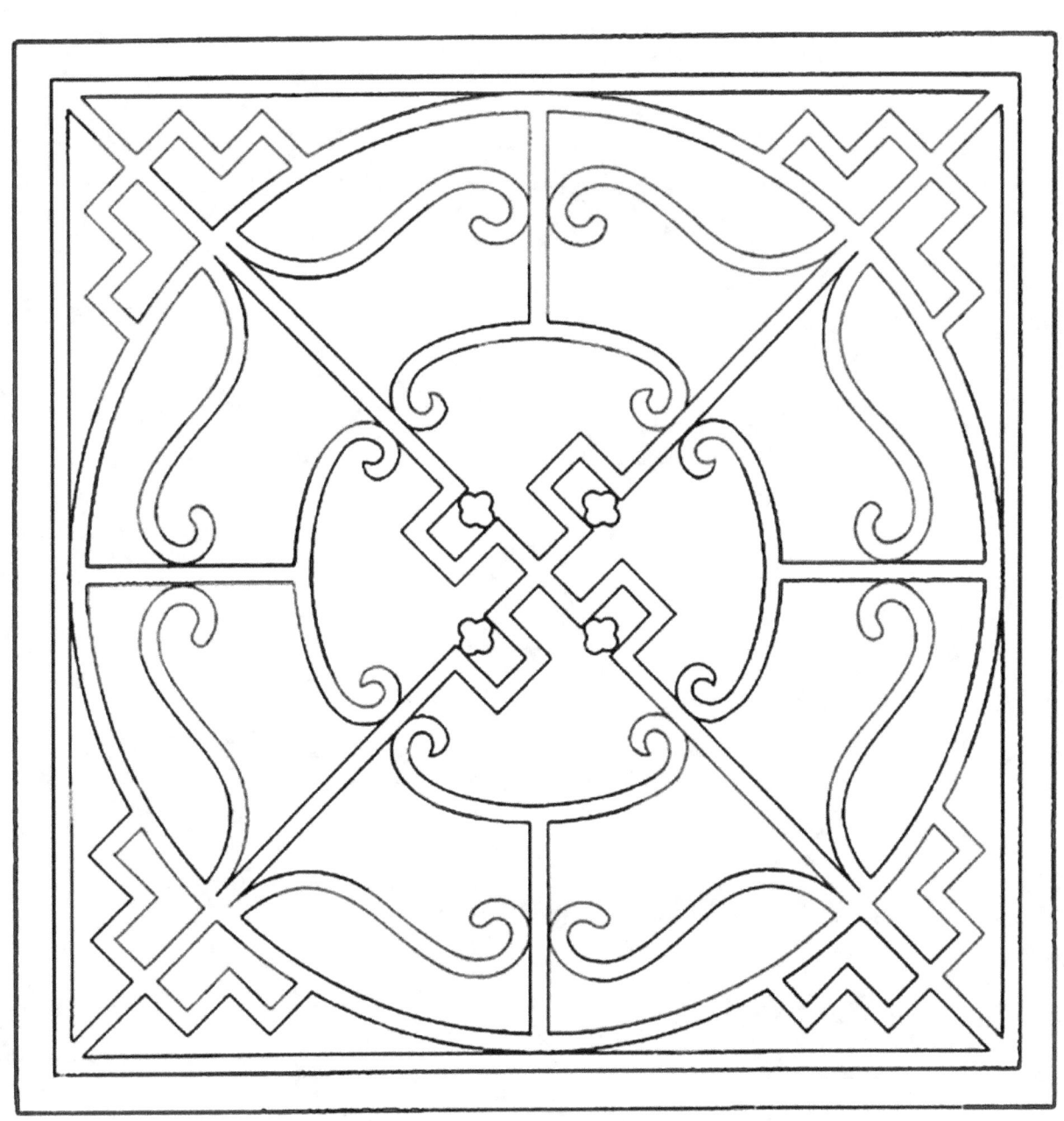

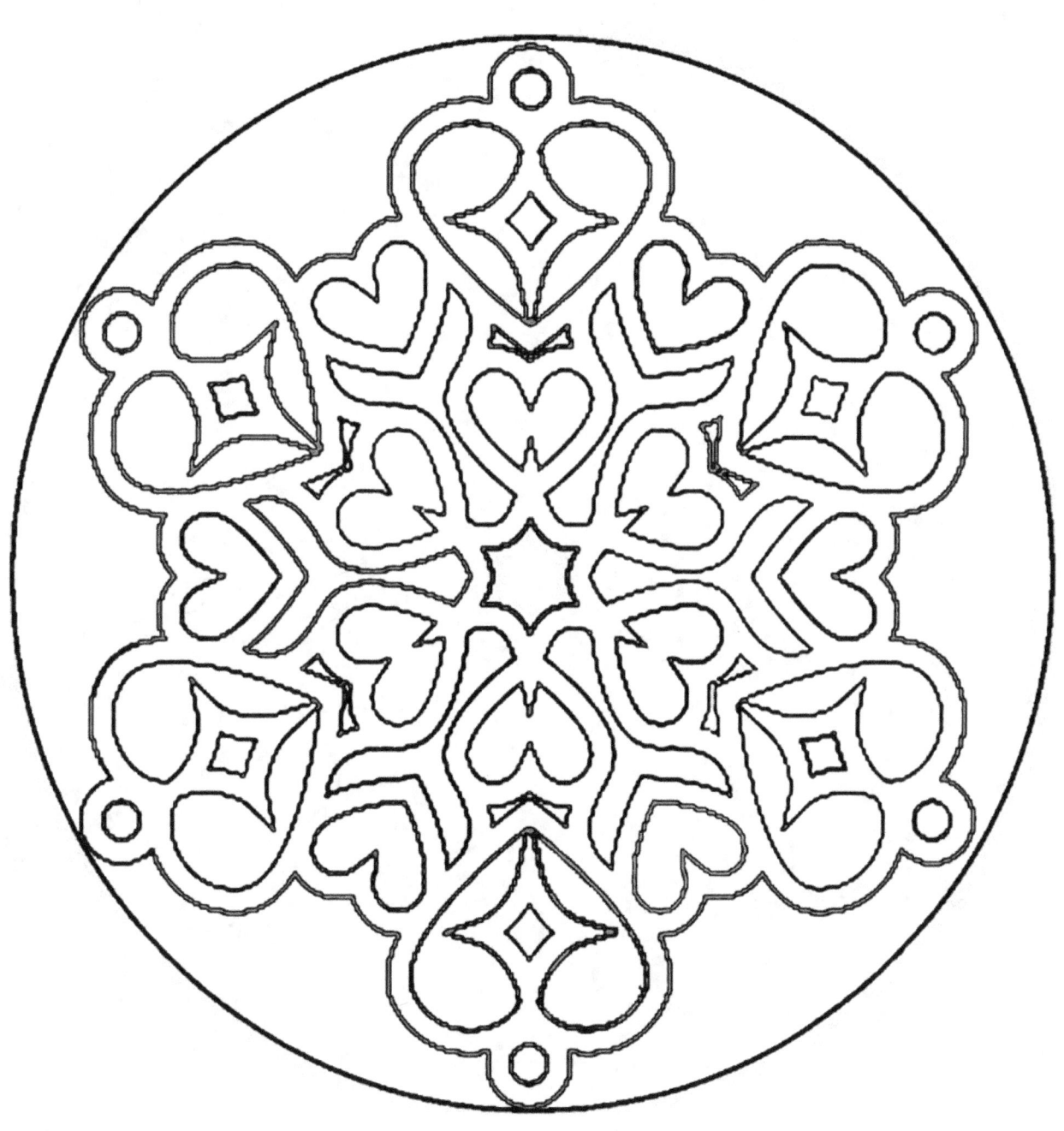

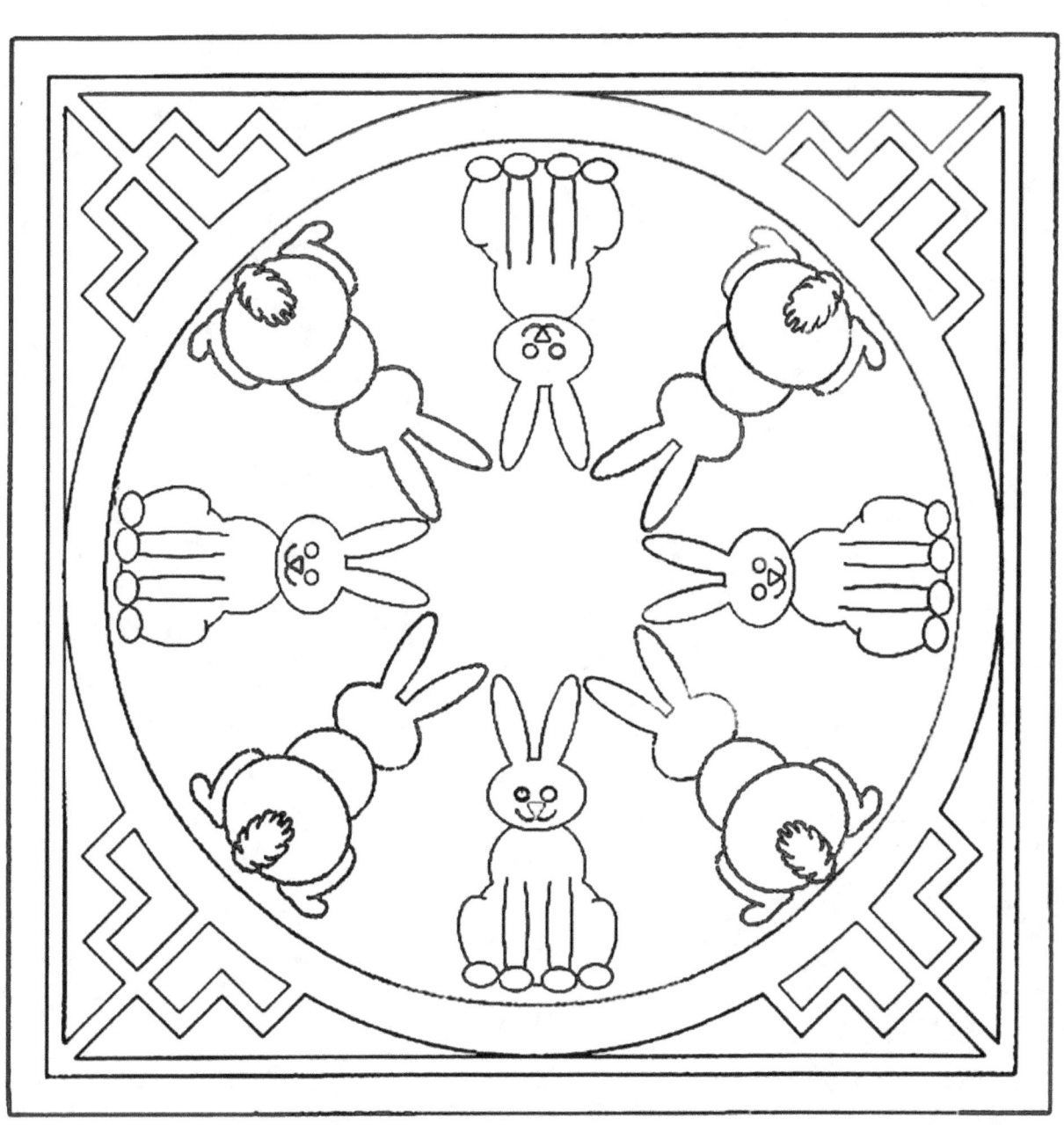

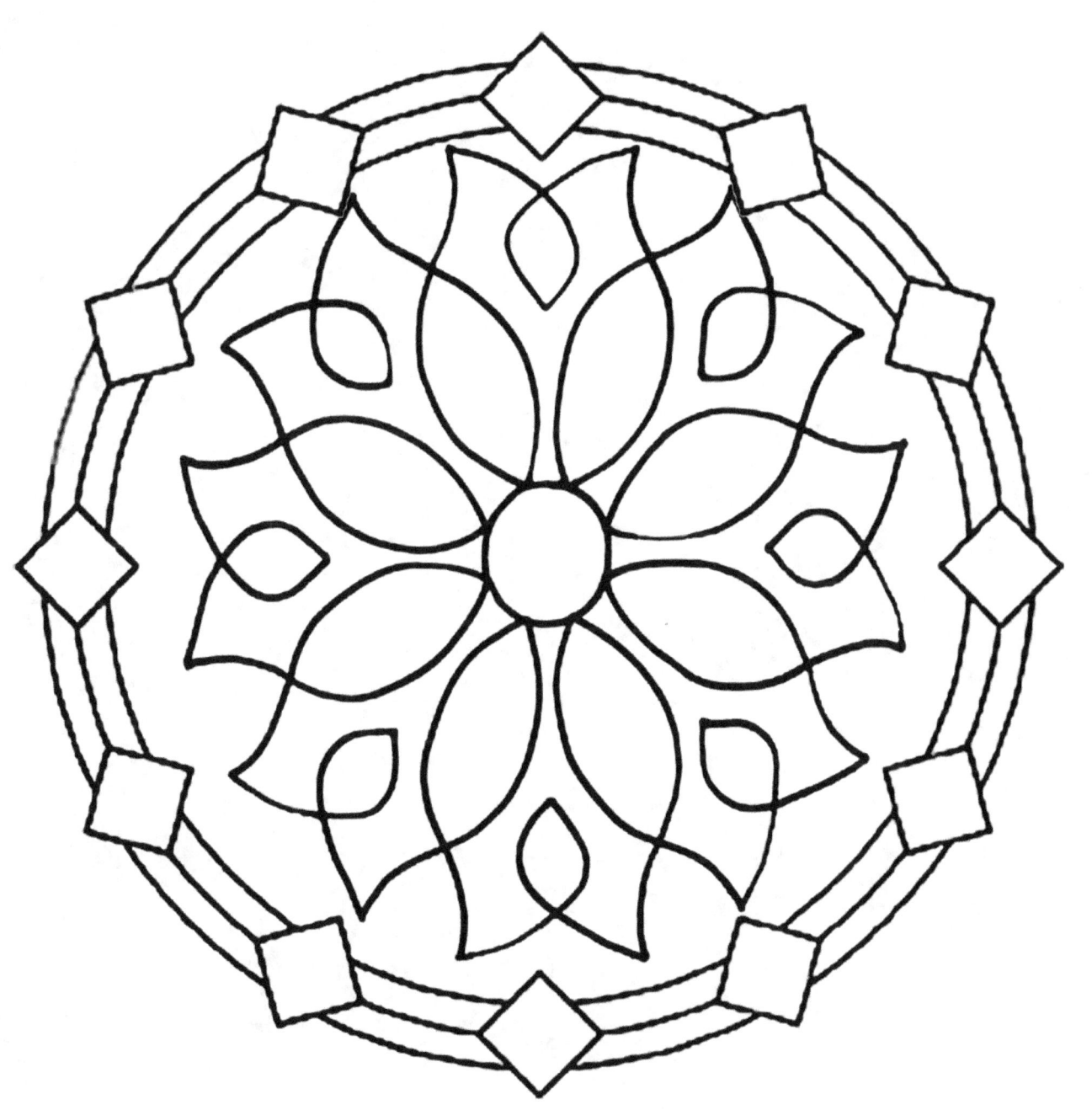

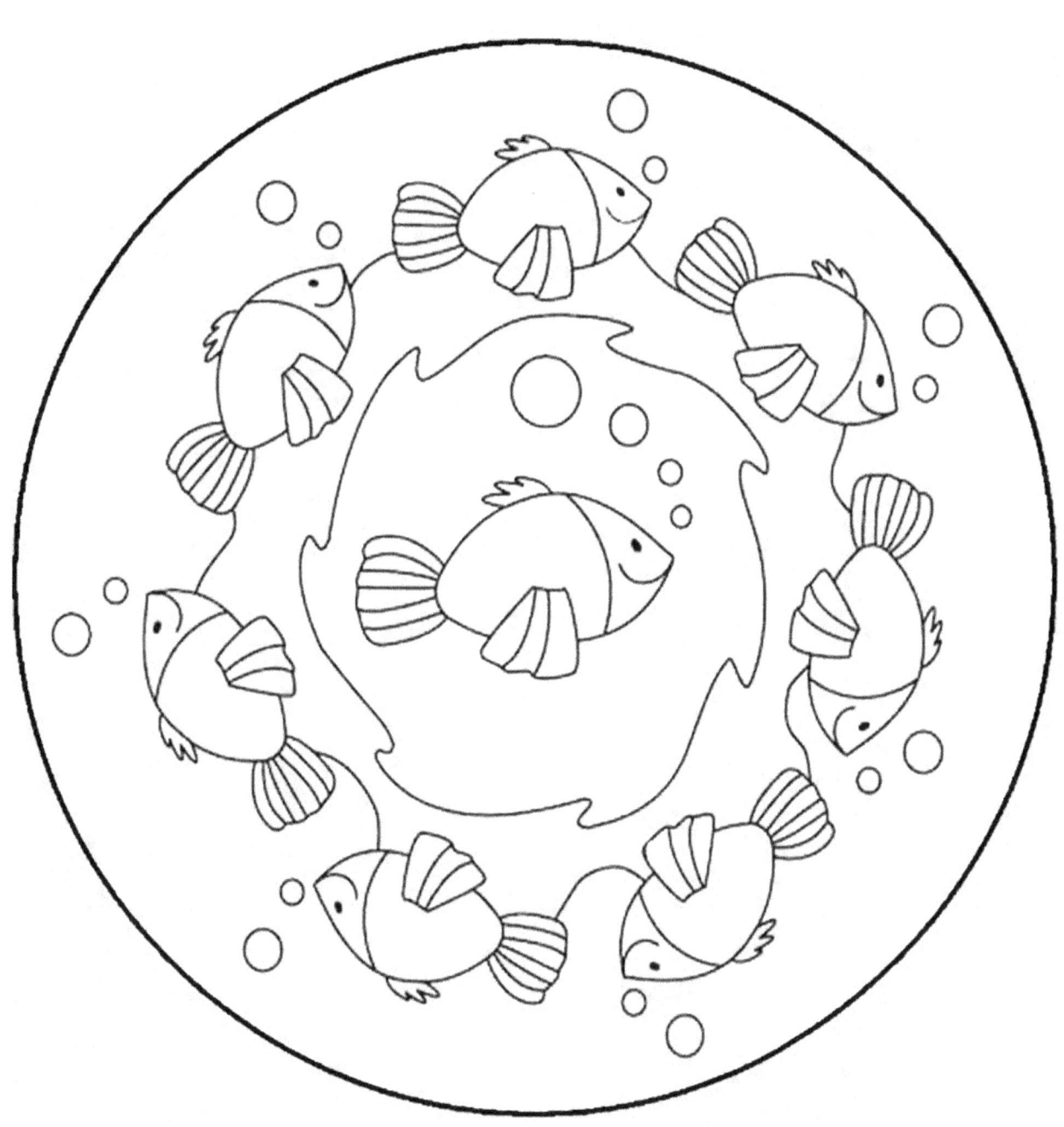

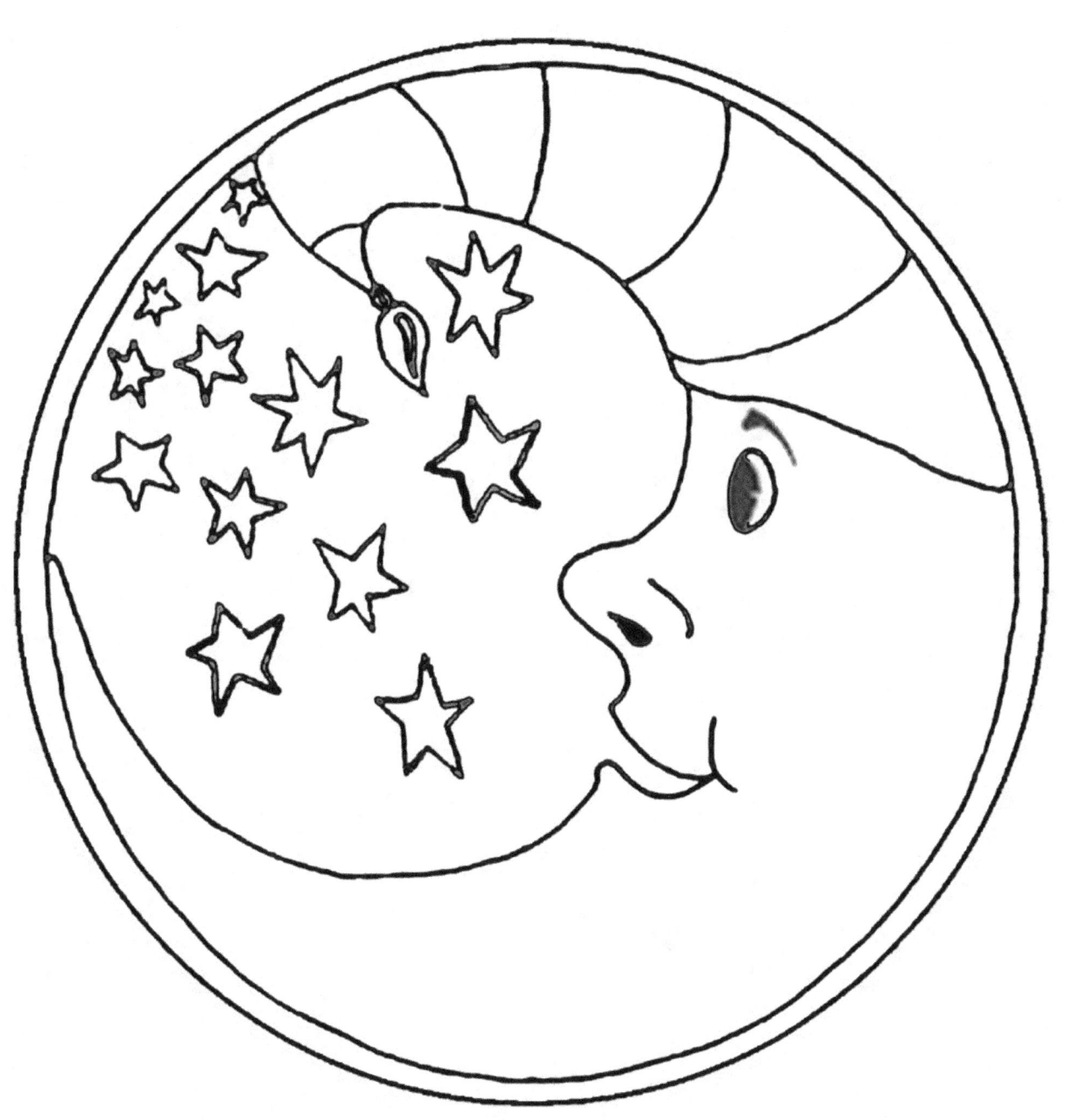

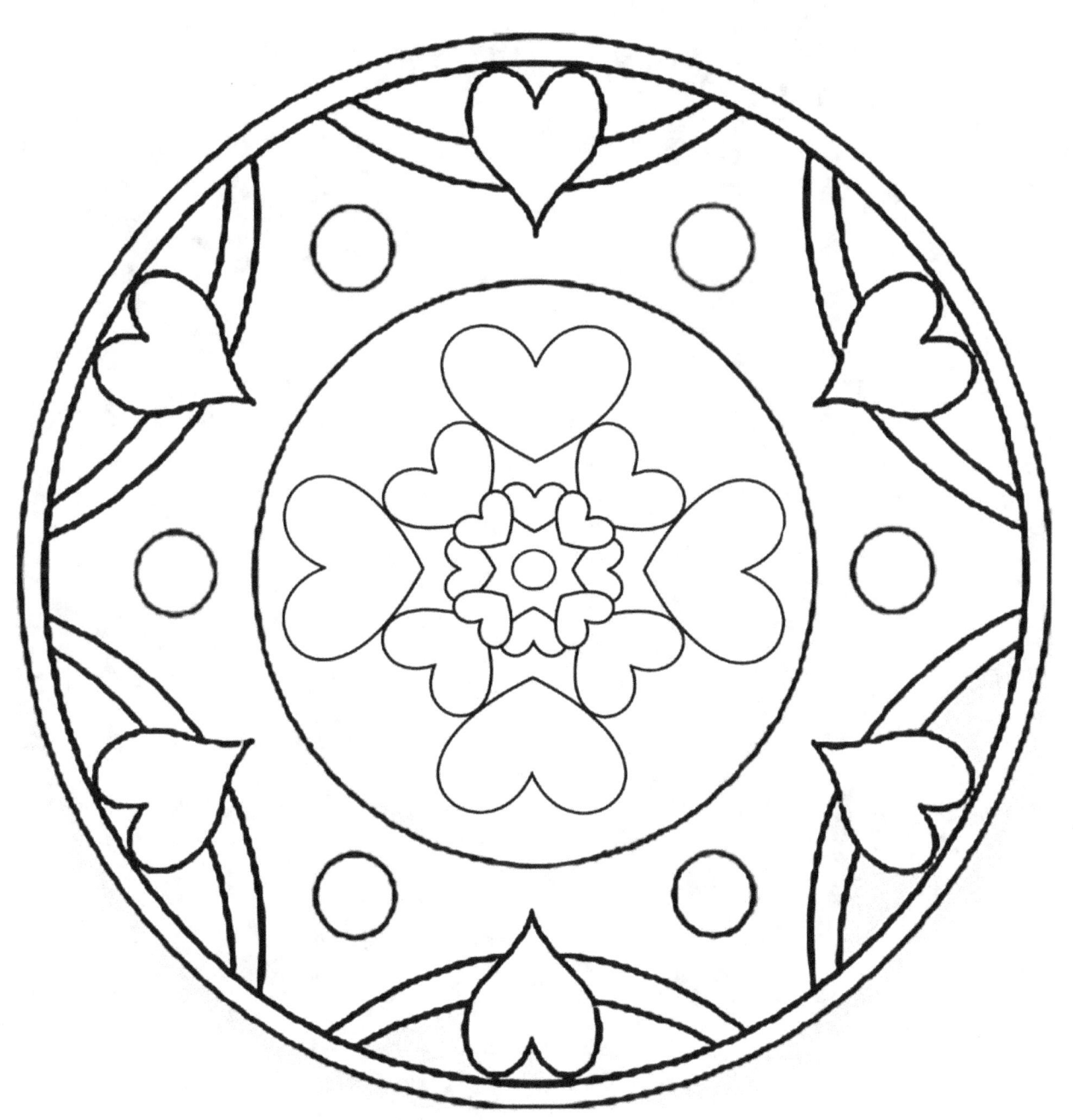

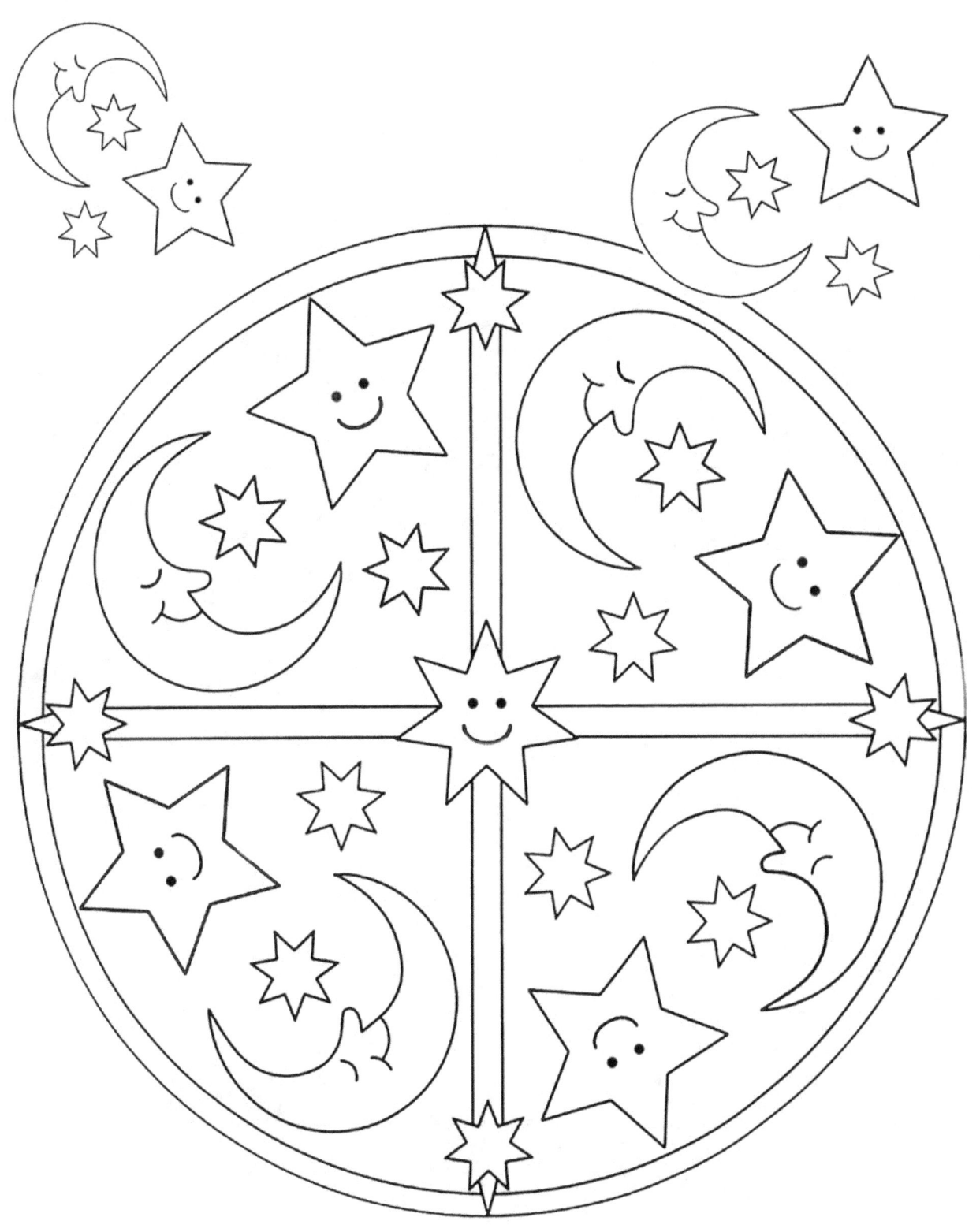

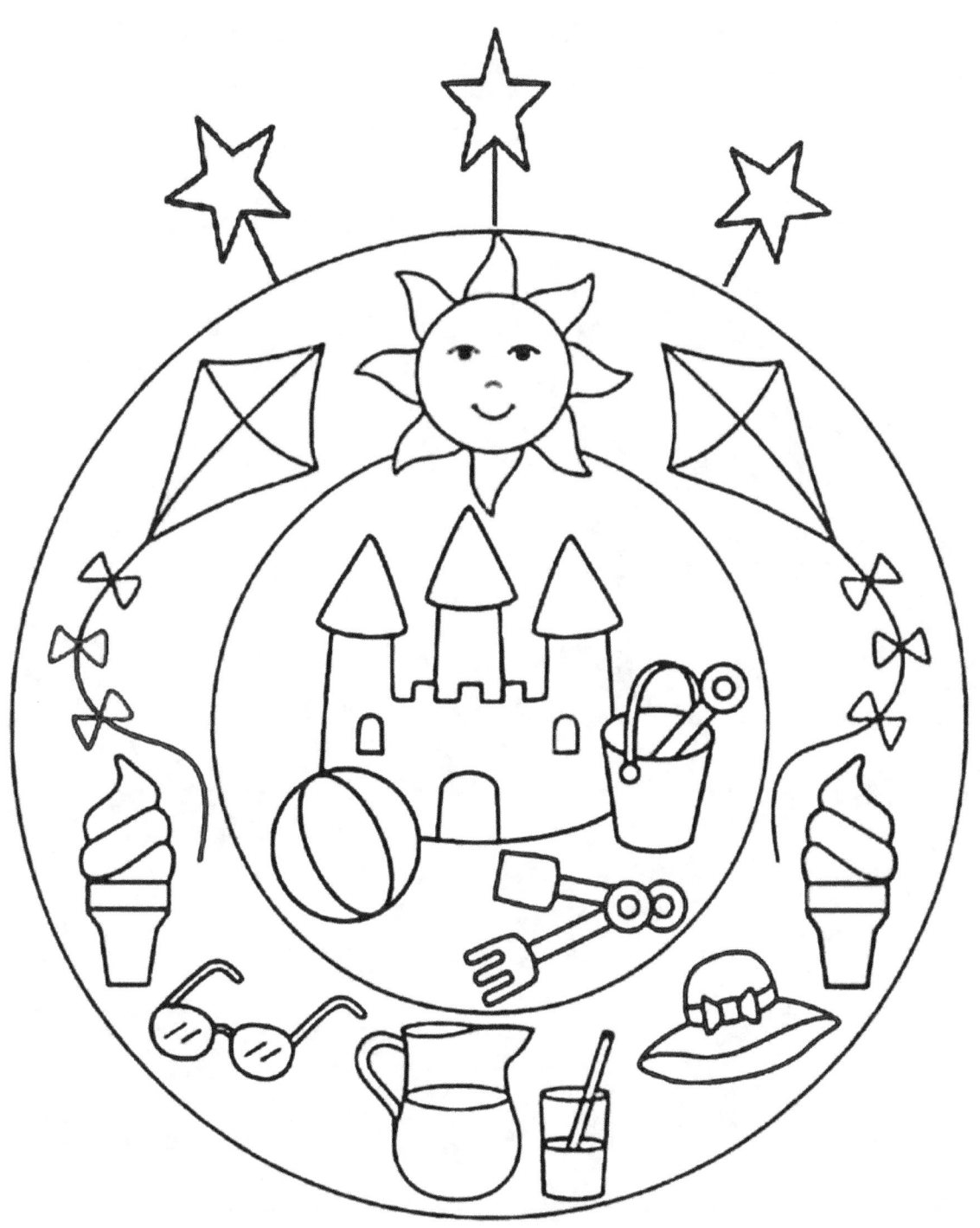

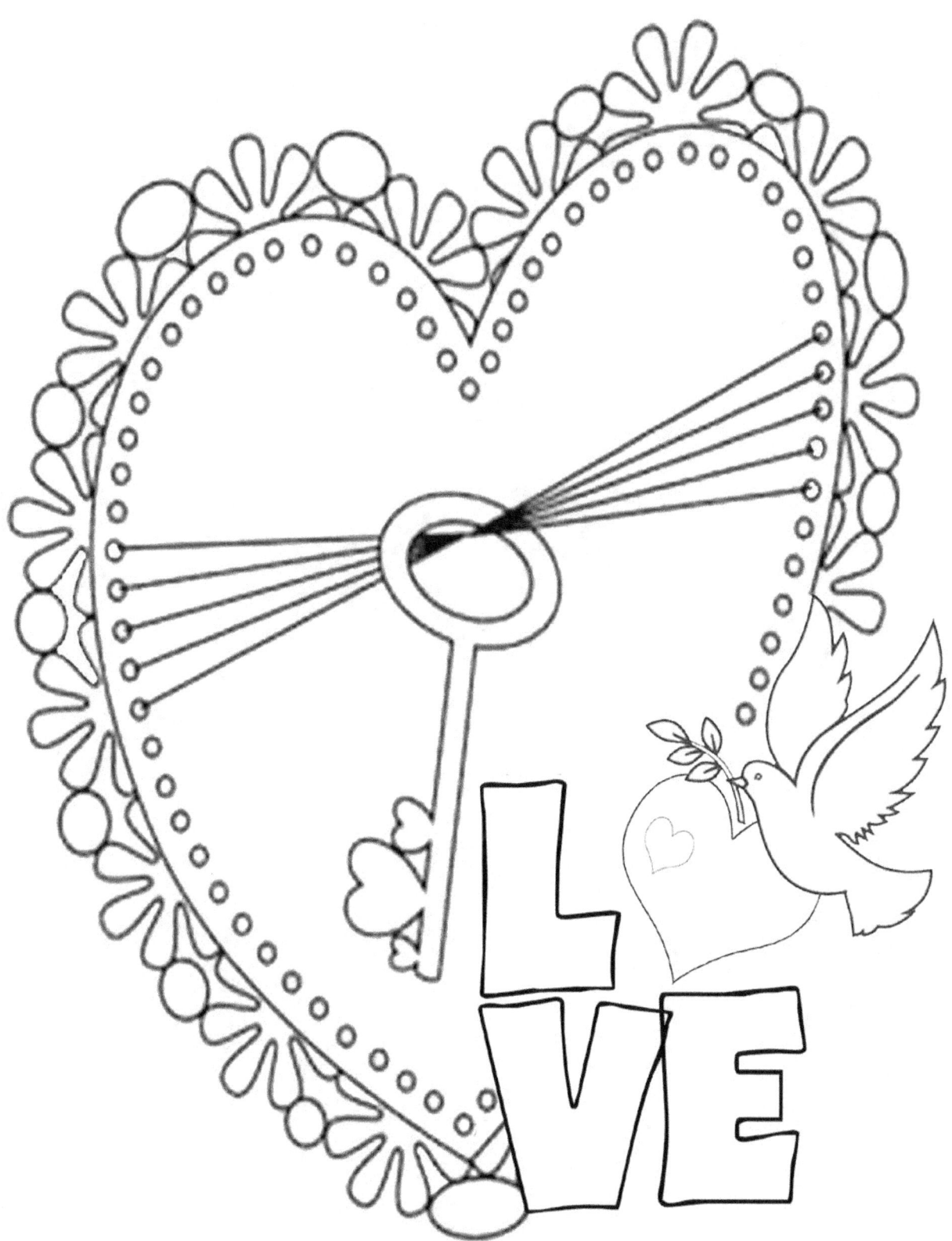

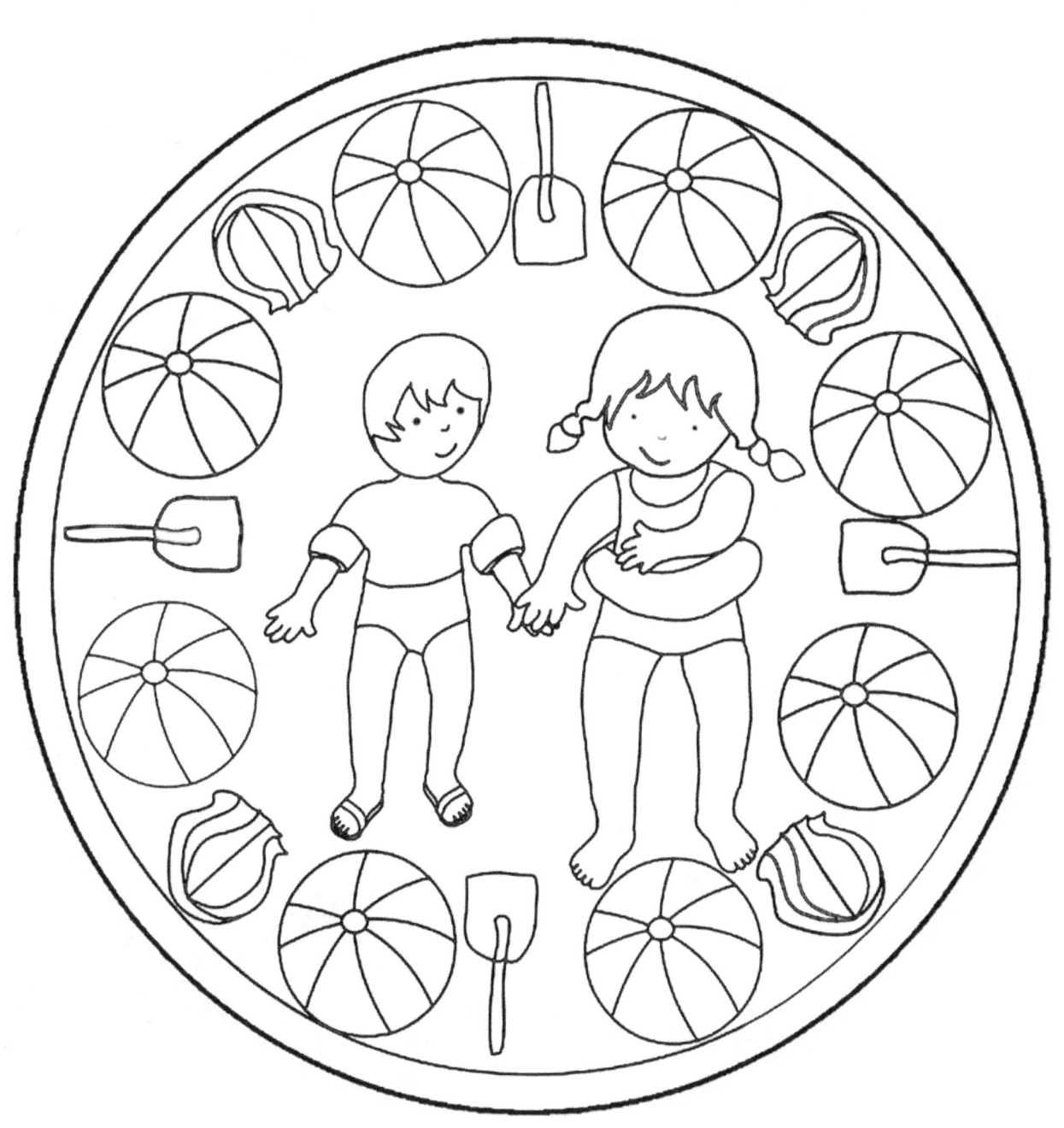

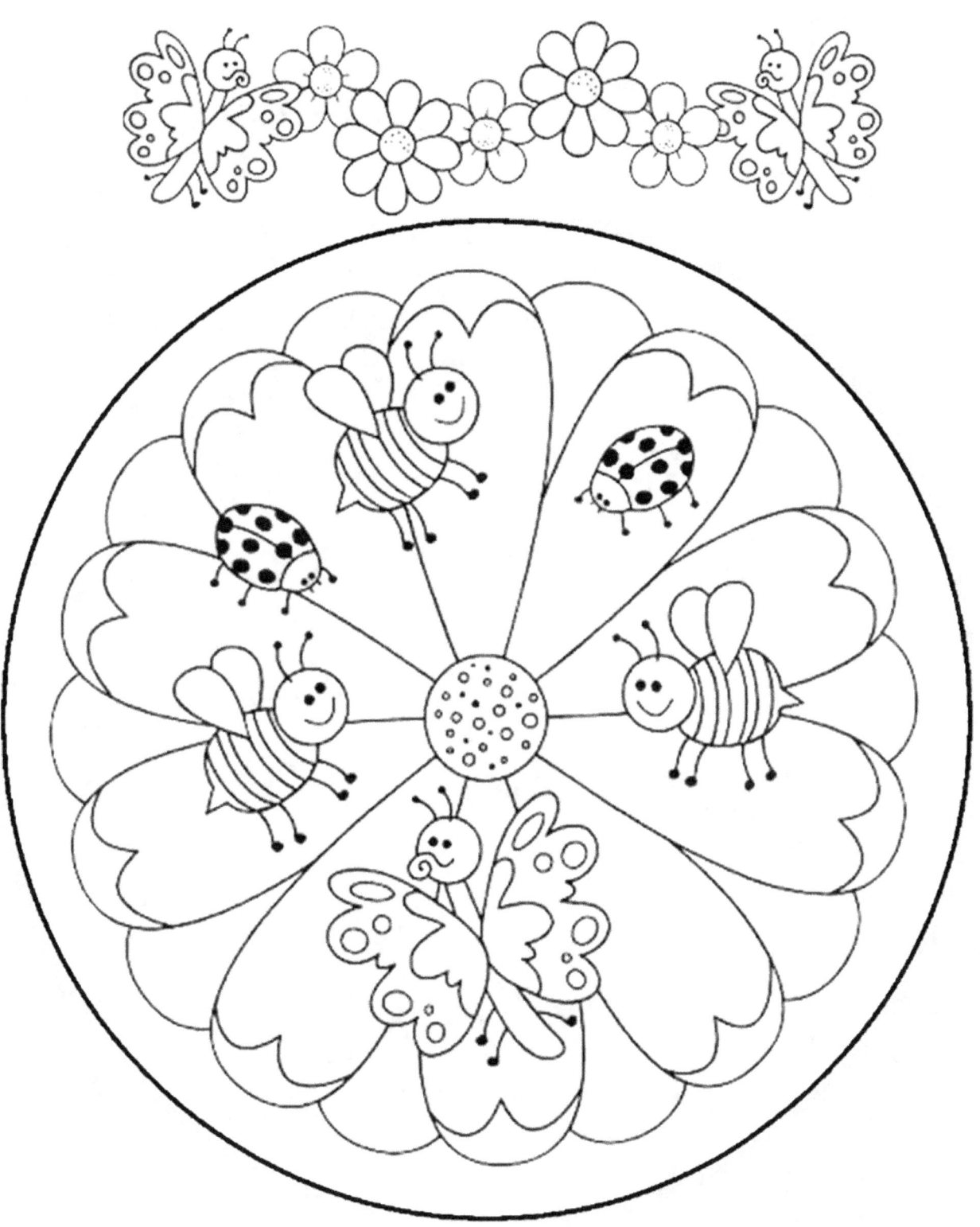

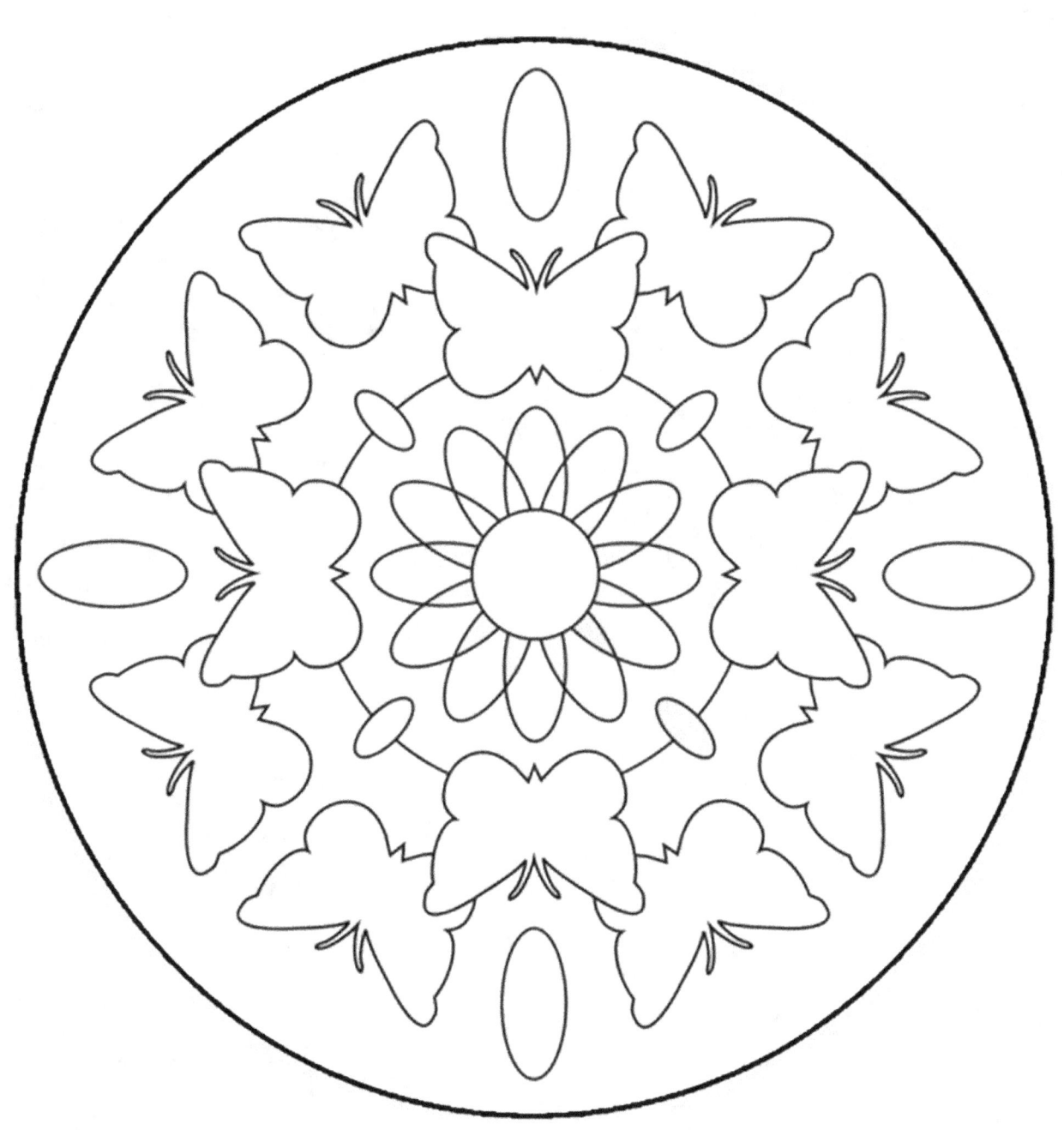

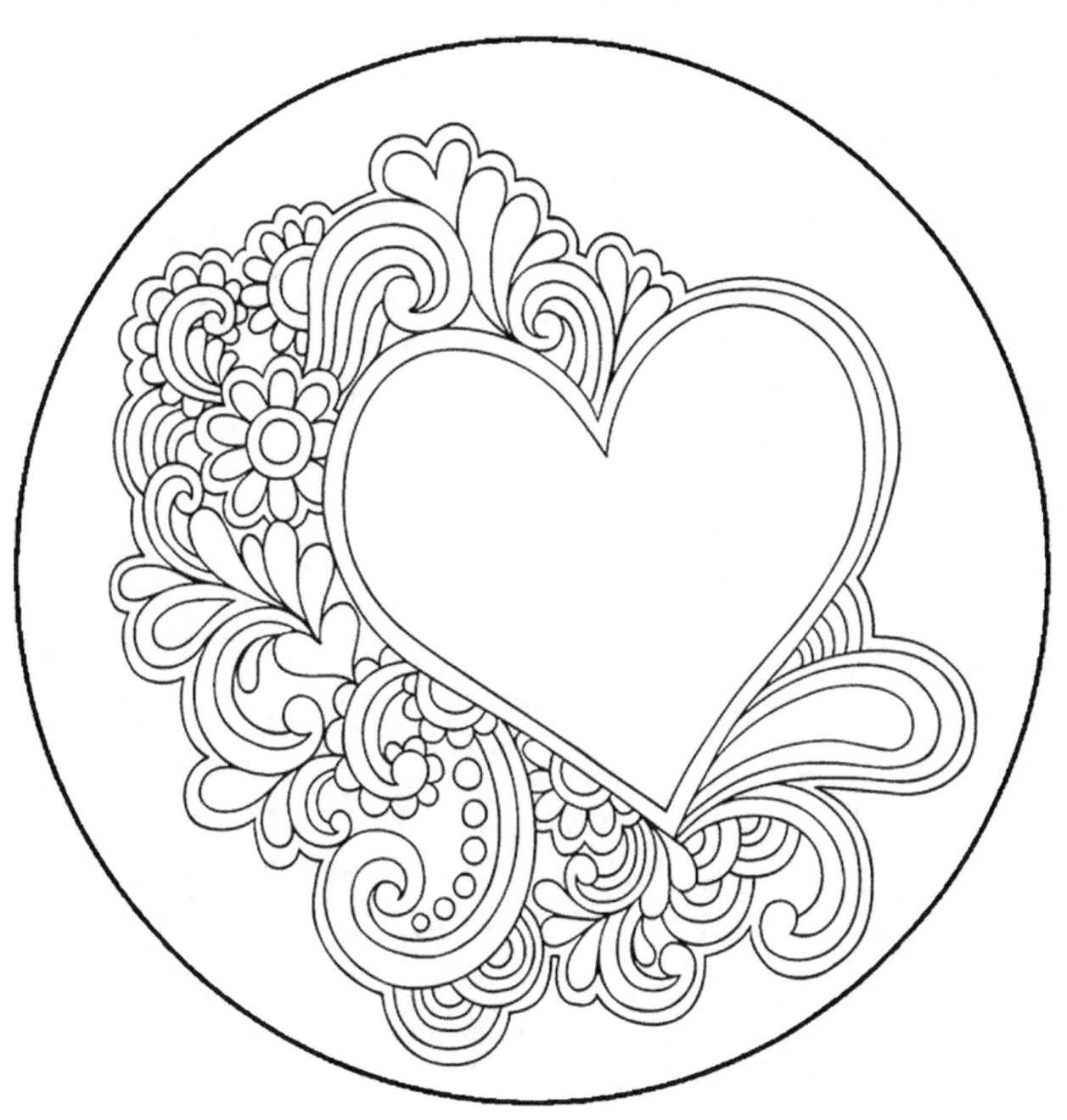

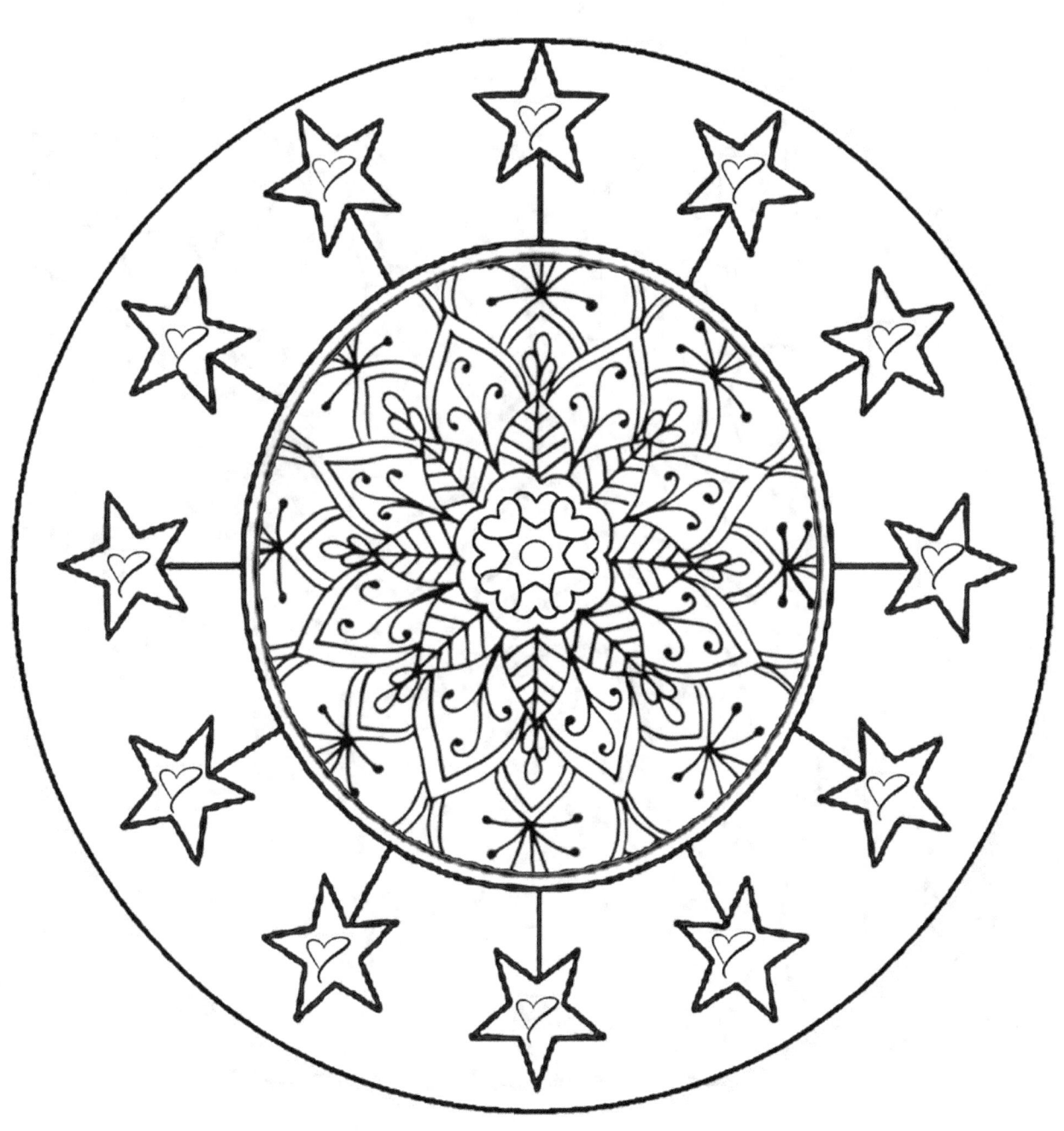

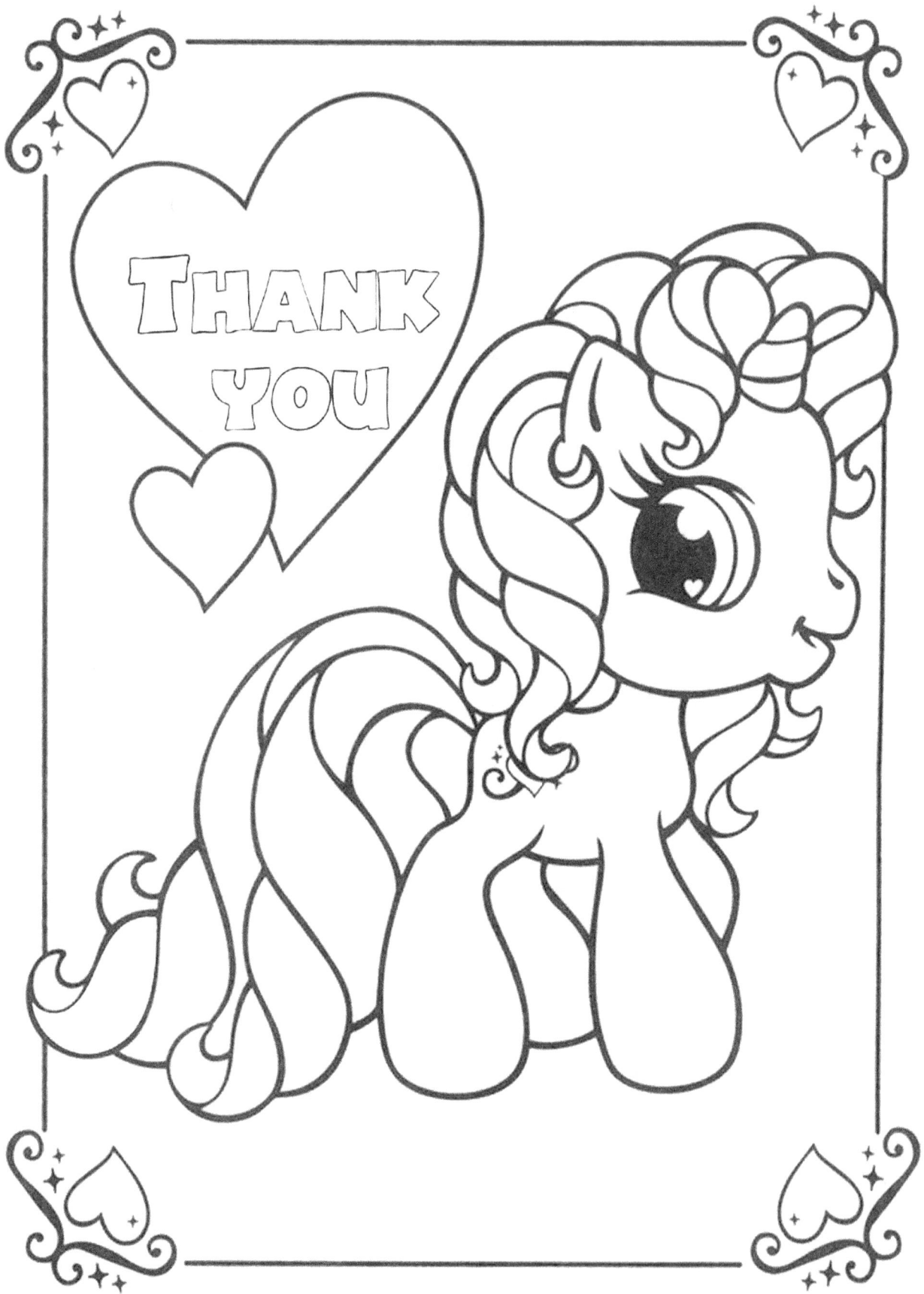

www.ingramcontent.com/pod-product-compliance
Lightning Source LLC
Chambersburg PA
CBHW081615220526
45468CB00010B/2885